1990

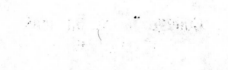

APOSTOLIC CONSTITUTION
EX CORDE ECCLESIAE
OF THE SUPREME PONTIFF

JOHN PAUL II
ON CATHOLIC UNIVERSITIES

378.01
JP II

Contents

138,253

Introduction

1. Born from the heart of the Church, a Catholic university is located in that course of tradition which may be traced back to the very origin of the university as an institution. It has always been recognized as an incomparable center of creativity and dissemination of knowledge for the good of humanity. By vocation, the *universitas magistrorum et scholarium* is dedicated to research, to teaching and to the education of students who freely associate with their teachers in a common love of knowledge.[1] With every other university it shares that *gaudium de veritate,* so precious to St. Augustine, which is that joy of searching for, discovering and communicating truth[2] in every field of knowledge. A Catholic university's privileged task is "to unite existentially by intellectual effort two orders of reality that too frequently tend to be placed in opposition as though they were antithetical: the search for truth, and the certainty of already knowing the fount of truth."[3]

2. For many years I myself was deeply enriched by the beneficial experience of university life: the ardent search for truth and its unselfish transmission to youth and to all those learning to think rigorously, so as to act rightly and to serve humanity better.

Therefore, I desire to share with everyone my profound respect for Catholic universities and to express my great appreciation for the work that is being done in them in the various spheres of knowledge. In a particular way, I wish to manifest my joy at the numerous meetings which the Lord has permitted me to have in the course of my apostolic journeys with the Catholic university communities of various continents. They are for me a lively and promising sign of the fecundity of the Christian mind in the heart of every culture. They give me a well-founded hope for a new flowering of Christian culture in the rich and varied context of our changing times, which certainly face serious challenges but which also bear so much promise under the action of the Spirit of truth and of love.

It is also my desire to express my pleasure and gratitude to the very many Catholic scholars engaged in teaching and research in non-Catholic universities. Their task as academics and scientists, lived out in the light of the Christian faith, is to be considered precious for the good of the universities in which they teach. Their presence, in fact, is a continuous stimulus to the selfless search for truth and for the wisdom that comes from above.

3. Since the beginning of this pontificate, I have shared these ideas and sentiments with my closest collaborators, the cardinals, with the Congregation for Catholic Education, and with men and women of culture throughout the world. In fact, the dialogue of the Church with the cultures of our times is that vital area where "the future of the Church and of the world is being played out as we conclude the 20th century."[4]

There is only one culture: that of man, by man and for man.[5] And thanks to her Catholic universities and their humanistic and scientific inheritance, the Church, expert in humanity, as my predecessor, Paul VI, expressed it at the United Nations,[6] explores the mysteries of humanity and of the world, clarifying them in the light of Revelation.

4. It is the honor and responsibility of a Catholic univer-

sity to consecrate itself without reserve to *the cause of truth.* This is its way of serving at one and the same time both the dignity of man and the good of the Church, which has "an intimate conviction that truth is [its] real ally...and that knowledge and reason are sure ministers to faith."[7] Without in any way neglecting the acquisition of useful knowledge, a Catholic university is distinguished by its free search for the whole truth about nature, man and God. The present age is in urgent need of this kind of disinterested service, namely of *proclaiming the meaning of truth,* that fundamental value without which freedom, justice and human dignity are extinguished. By means of a kind of universal humanism a Catholic university is completely dedicated to the research of all aspects of truth in their essential connection with the supreme Truth, who is God. It does this without fear but rather with enthusiasm, dedicating itself to every path of knowledge, aware of being preceded by him who is "the Way, the Truth, and the Life,"[8] the *Logos,* whose Spirit of intelligence and love enables the human person with his or her own intelligence to find the ultimate reality of which he is the source and end and who alone is capable of giving fully that Wisdom without which the future of the world would be in danger.

5. It is in the context of the impartial search for truth that the relationship between faith and reason is brought to light and meaning. The invitation of St. Augustine, *"Intellege ut credas; crede ut intellegas,"*[9] is relevant to Catholic universities that are called to explore courageously the riches of Revelation and of nature so that the united endeavor of intelligence and faith will enable people to come to the full measure of their humanity, created in the image and likeness of God, renewed even more marvelously after sin, in Christ, and called to shine forth in the light of the Spirit.

6. Through the encounter which it establishes between the

unfathomable richness of the salvific message of the Gospel and the variety and immensity of the fields of knowledge in which that richness is incarnated by it, a Catholic university enables the Church to institute an incomparably fertile dialogue with people of every culture. Man's life is given dignity by culture, and, while he finds his fullness in Christ, there can be no doubt that the Gospel, which reaches and renews him in every dimension, is also fruitful for the culture in which he lives.

7. In the world today, characterized by such rapid developments in science and technology, the tasks of a Catholic university assume an ever greater importance and urgency. Scientific and technological discoveries create an enormous economic and industrial growth, but they also inescapably require the correspondingly necessary *search for meaning* in order to guarantee that the new discoveries be used for the authentic good of individuals and of human society as a whole. If it is the responsibility of every university to search for such meaning, a Catholic university is called in a particular way to respond to this need: Its Christian inspiration enables it to include the moral, spiritual and religious dimension in its research, and to evaluate the attainments of science and technology in the perspective of the totality of the human person.

In this context Catholic universities are called to a continuous renewal, both as "universities" and as "Catholic." For "what is at stake is the *very meaning of scientific and technological research, of social life and of culture,* but, on an even more profound level, what is at stake is *the very meaning of the human person.*"[10] Such renewal requires a clear awareness that, by its Catholic character, a university is made more capable of conducting an *impartial* search for truth, a search that is neither subordinated to nor conditioned by particular interests of any kind.

8. Having already dedicated the Apostolic Constitution *Sapientia Christiana* to ecclesiastical faculties and universities,[11] I then felt obliged to propose an analogous document for Catholic universities as a sort of "magna carta," enriched by the long and fruitful experience of the Church in the realm of universities and open to the promise of future achievements that will require courageous creativity and rigorous fidelity.

9. The present document is addressed especially to those who conduct Catholic universities, to the respective academic communities, to all those who have an interest in them, particularly the bishops, religious congregations and ecclesial *institutions*, and to the numerous laity who are committed to the great mission of higher education. Its purpose is that "the Christian mind may achieve, as it were, a public, persistent and universal presence in the whole enterprise of advancing higher culture and that the students of these institutions become people outstanding in learning, ready to shoulder society's heavier burdens and to witness the faith to the world."[12]

10. In addition to Catholic universities, I also turn to the many Catholic institutions of higher education. According to their nature and proper objectives, they share some or all of the characteristics of a university and they offer their own contribution to the Church and to society, whether through research, education or professional training. While this document specifically concerns Catholic universities, it is also meant to include all Catholic institutions of higher education engaged in instilling the Gospel message of Christ in souls and cultures.

Therefore, it is with great trust and hope that I invite all Catholic universities to pursue their irreplaceable task. Their mission appears increasingly necessary for the encounter of the Church with the development of the sciences and with the cultures of our age.

Together with all my brother bishops who share pastoral responsibility with me, I would like to manifest my deep conviction that a Catholic university is without any doubt one of the best instruments that the Church offers to our age, which is searching for certainty and wisdom. Having the mission of bringing the Good News to everyone, the Church should never fail to interest herself in this institution. By research and teaching, Catholic universities assist the Church in the manner most appropriate to modern times to find cultural treasures both old and new, *"nova et vetera,"* according to the words of Jesus.[13]

11. Finally, I turn to the whole Church, convinced that Catholic universities are essential to her growth and to the development of Christian culture and human progress. For this reason, the entire ecclesial community is invited to give its support to Catholic institutions of higher education and to assist them in their process of development and renewal. It is invited in a special way to guard the rights and freedom of these institutions in civil society, and to offer them economic aid, especially in those countries where they have more urgent need of it, and to furnish assistance in founding new Catholic universities wherever this might be necessary.

My hope is that these prescriptions, based on the teaching of Vatican Council II and the directives of the Code of Canon Law, will enable Catholic universities and other institutes of higher studies to fulfill their indispensable mission in the new advent of grace that is opening up to the new millennium.

Part I:
Identity and Mission

A. The Identity of a Catholic University

1. Nature and Objectives

12. Every Catholic university, *as a university,* is an academic community which, in a rigorous and critical fashion, assists in the protection and advancement of human dignity and of a cultural heritage through research, teaching and various services offered to the local, national and international communities.[14] It possesses that institutional autonomy necessary to perform its functions effectively and guarantees its members academic freedom, so long as the rights of the individual person and of the community are preserved within the confines of the truth and the common good.[15]

13. Since the objective of a Catholic university is to assure in an institutional manner a Christian presence in the university world confronting the great problems of society and culture,[16] every Catholic university, as *Catholic,* must have the following *essential characteristics:*

"1. A Christian inspiration not only of individuals but of the university community as such;

"2. A continuing reflection in the light of the Catholic faith upon the growing treasury of human knowledge, to which it seeks to contribute by its own research;

"3. Fidelity to the Christian message as it comes to us through the Church;

"4. An institutional commitment to the service of the people of God and of the human family in their pilgrimage to the transcendent goal which gives meaning to life."[17]

14. "In the light of these four characteristics, it is evident that besides the teaching, research and services common to all universities, a Catholic university, *by institutional commitment,* brings to its task the inspiration and light of the *Christian message.* In a Catholic university, therefore, Catholic ideals, attitudes and principles penetrate and inform university activities in accordance with the proper nature and autonomy of these activities. In a word, being both a university and Catholic, it must be both a community of scholars representing various branches of human knowledge, and an academic institution in which Catholicism is vitally present and operative."[18]

15. A Catholic university, therefore, is a place of research, where scholars *scrutinize reality* with the methods proper to each academic discipline, and so contribute to the treasury of human knowledge. Each individual discipline is studied in a systematic manner; moreover, the various disciplines are brought into dialogue for their mutual enhancement.

In addition to assisting men and women in their continuing quest for the truth, this research provides an effective witness, especially necessary today, to the Church's belief in the intrinsic value of knowledge and research.

In a Catholic university, research necessarily includes (a) the search for an *integration of knowledge,* (b) a *dialogue between faith and reason,* (c) an *ethical concern,* and (d) a *theological perspective.*

16. *Integration of knowledge* is a process, one which will always remain incomplete; moreover, the explosion of knowledge in recent decades, together with the rigid compartmentalization of knowledge within individual academic disciplines, makes the task increasingly difficult. But a university, and especially a Catholic university, *"has to be a 'living union' of individual organisms* dedicated to the search for

truth.... It is necessary *to work toward a higher synthesis* of knowledge, in which alone lies the possibility of satisfying that thirst for truth which is profoundly inscribed on the heart of the human person."[19] Aided by the specific contributions of philosophy and theology, university scholars will be engaged in a constant effort to determine the relative place and meaning of each of the various disciplines within the context of a vision of the human person and the world that is enlightened by the Gospel, and therefore by a faith in Christ, the *Logos,* as the center of creation and of human history.

17. In promoting this integration of knowledge, a specific part of a Catholic university's task is to promote *dialogue between faith and reason,* so that it can be seen more profoundly how faith and reason bear harmonious witness to the unity of all truth. While each academic discipline retains its own integrity and has its own methods, this dialogue demonstrates that "methodical research within every branch of learning, when carried out in a truly scientific manner and in accord with moral norms, can never truly conflict with faith. For the things of the earth and the concerns of faith derive from the same God."[20] A vital interaction of two distinct levels of coming to know the one truth leads to a greater love for truth itself, and contributes to a more comprehensive understanding of the meaning of human life and of the purpose of God's creation.

18. Because knowledge is meant to serve the human person, research in a Catholic university is always carried out with a concern for the *ethical* and *moral implications* both of its methods and of its discoveries. This concern, while it must be present in all research, is particularly important in the areas of science and technology. "It is essential that we be convinced of the priority of the ethical over the technical, of the primacy of the person over things, of the superiority of the

spirit over matter. The cause of the human person will only be served if knowledge is joined to conscience. Men and women of science will truly aid humanity only if they preserve 'the sense of the transcendence of the human person over the world and of God over the human person.' "[21]

19. *Theology* plays a particularly important role in the search for a synthesis of knowledge as well as in the dialogue between faith and reason. It serves all other disciplines in their search for meaning, not only by helping them to investigate how their discoveries will affect individuals and society but also by bringing a perspective and an orientation not contained within their own methodologies. In turn, interaction with these other disciplines and their discoveries enriches theology, offering it a better understanding of the world today, and making theological research more relevant to current needs. Because of its specific importance among the academic disciplines, every Catholic university should have a faculty, or at least a chair, of theology.[22]

20. Given the close connection between research and teaching, the research qualities indicated above will have their influence on all teaching. While each discipline is taught systematically and according to its own methods, *interdisciplinary studies,* assisted by a careful and thorough study of philosophy and theology, enable students to acquire an organic vision of reality and to develop a continuing desire for intellectual progress. In the communication of knowledge, emphasis is then placed on how *human reason in its reflection* opens to increasingly broader questions and how the complete answer to them can only come from above through faith. Furthermore, the *moral implications* that are present in each discipline are examined as an integral part of the teaching of that discipline so that the entire educative process be directed toward the whole development of the person. Finally, Catho-

lic theology, taught in a manner faithful to Scripture, Tradition and the Church's Magisterium, provides an awareness of the Gospel principles which will enrich the meaning of human life and give it a new dignity.

Through research and teaching the students are educated in the various disciplines so as to become truly competent in the specific sectors in which they will devote themselves to the service of society and of the Church, but at the same time prepared to give the witness of their faith to the world.

2. The University Community

21. A Catholic university pursues its objectives through its formation of an authentic human community animated by the spirit of Christ. The source of its unity springs from a common dedication to the truth, a common vision of the dignity of the human person and, ultimately, the person and message of Christ, which gives the institution its distinctive character. As a result of this inspiration, the community is animated by a spirit of freedom and charity; it is characterized by mutual respect, sincere dialogue, and protection of the rights of individuals. It assists each of its members to achieve wholeness as human persons; in turn, everyone in the community helps in promoting unity, and each one, according to his or her role and capacity, contributes toward decisions which affect the community and also toward maintaining and strengthening the distinctive Catholic character of the institution.

22. *University teachers* should seek to improve their competence and endeavor to set the content, objectives, methods and results of research in an individual discipline within the framework of a coherent world vision. Christians among the teachers are called to be witnesses and educators of authentic Christian life, which evidences an attained inte-

gration between faith and life, and between professional competence and Christian wisdom. All teachers are to be inspired by academic ideals and by the principles of an authentically human life.

23. *Students* are challenged to pursue an education that combines excellence in humanistic and cultural development with specialized professional training. Most especially, they are challenged to continue the search for truth and for meaning throughout their lives, since "the human spirit must be cultivated in such a way that there results a growth in its ability to wonder, to understand, to contemplate, to make personal judgments, and to develop a religious, moral and social sense."[23] This enables them to acquire or, if they have already done so, to deepen a Christian way of life that is authentic. They should realize the responsibility of their professional life, the enthusiasm of being the trained "leaders" of tomorrow, of being witnesses to Christ in whatever place they may exercise their profession.

24. *Directors and administrators* in a Catholic university promote the constant growth of the university and its community through a leadership of service; the dedication and witness of the *non-academic staff* are vital for the identity and life of the university.

25. Many Catholic universities were founded by religious congregations, and continue to depend on their support; those religious congregations dedicated to the apostolate of higher education are urged to assist these institutions in the renewal of their commitment and to continue to prepare religious men and women who can positively contribute to the mission of a Catholic university.

Lay people have found in university activities a means by which they too could exercise an important apostolic role in the Church, and, in most Catholic universities today the academic community is largely composed of laity; in increasing numbers, lay men and women are assuming important functions and responsibilities for the direction of these institutions. These lay Catholics are responding to the Church's call "to be present, as signs of courage and intellectual creativity, in the privileged places of culture, that is, the world of education— school and university."[24] The future of Catholic universities depends to a great extent on the competent and dedicated service of lay Catholics. The Church sees their developing presence in these institutions both as a sign of hope and as a confirmation of the irreplaceable lay vocation in the Church and in the world, confident that lay people will, in the exercise of their own distinctive role, "illumine and organize these [temporal] affairs in such a way that they always start out, develop, and continue according to Christ's mind, to the praise of the Creator and the Redeemer."[25]

26. The university community of many Catholic institutions includes members of other churches, ecclesial communities and religions, and also those who profess no religious belief. These men and women offer their training and experience in furthering the various academic disciplines or other university tasks.

3. *The Catholic University in the Church*

27. Every Catholic university, without ceasing to be a university, has a relationship to the Church that is essential to its institutional identity. As such, it participates most directly in the life of the local Church in which it is situated; at the same time, because it is an academic institution and therefore a part of the international community of scholarship and inquiry, each institution participates in and contributes to the life and the mission of the universal Church, assuming consequently a special bond with the Holy See by reason of the

service to unity which it is called to render to the whole Church. One consequence of its essential relationship to the Church is that the *institutional* fidelity of the university to the Christian message includes a recognition of and adherence to the teaching authority of the Church in matters of faith and morals. Catholic members of the university community are also called to a personal fidelity to the Church with all that this implies. Non-Catholic members are required to respect the Catholic character of the university, while the university in turn respects their religious liberty.[26]

28. Bishops have a particular responsibility to promote Catholic universities, and especially to promote and assist in the preservation and strengthening of their Catholic identity, including the protection of their Catholic identity in relation to civil authorities. This will be achieved more effectively if close personal and pastoral relationships exist between university and Church authorities characterized by mutual trust, close and consistent cooperation and continuing dialogue. Even when they do not enter directly into the internal governance of the university, bishops "should be seen not as external agents but as participants in the life of the Catholic university."[27]

29. The Church, accepting "the legitimate autonomy of human culture and especially of the sciences," recognizes the academic freedom of scholars in each discipline in accordance with its own principles and proper methods,[28] and within the confines of the truth and the common good.

Theology has its legitimate place in the university alongside other disciplines. It has proper principles and methods which define it as a branch of knowledge. Theologians enjoy this same freedom so long as they are faithful to these principles and methods.

Bishops should encourage the creative work of theologians. They serve the Church through research done in a way that respects theological method. They seek to understand better, further develop and more effectively communicate the meaning of Christian Revelation as transmitted in Scripture and Tradition and in the Church's Magisterium. They also investigate the ways in which theology can shed light on specific questions raised by contemporary culture. At the same time, since theology seeks an understanding of revealed truth whose authentic interpretation is entrusted to the bishops of the Church,[29] it is intrinsic to the principles and methods of their research and teaching in their academic discipline that theologians respect the authority of the bishops, and assent to Catholic doctrine according to the degree of authority with which it is taught.[30] Because of their interrelated roles, dialogue between bishops and theologians is essential; this is especially true today, when the results of research are so quickly and so widely communicated through the media.[31]

B. The Mission of Service of a Catholic University

30. The basic mission of a university is a continuous quest for truth through its research, and the preservation and communication of knowledge for the good of society. A Catholic university participates in this mission with its own specific characteristics and purposes.

1. Service to Church and Society

31. Through teaching and research, a Catholic university offers an indispensable contribution to the Church. In fact, it prepares men and women who, inspired by Christian princi-

ples and helped to live their Christian vocation in a mature and responsible manner, will be able to assume positions of responsibility in the Church. Moreover, by offering the results of its scientific research, a Catholic university will be able to help the Church respond to the problems and needs of this age.

32. A Catholic university, as any university, is immersed in human society; as an extension of its service to the Church and always within its proper competence, it is called on to become an ever more effective instrument of cultural progress for individuals as well as for society. Included among its research activities, therefore, will be a study of *serious contemporary problems* in areas such as the dignity of human life, the promotion of justice for all, the quality of personal and family life, the protection of nature, the search for peace and political stability, a more just sharing in the world's resources, and a new economic and political order that will better serve the human community at a national and international level. University research will seek to discover the roots and causes of the serious problems of our time, paying special attention to their ethical and religious dimensions.

If need be, a Catholic university must have the courage to speak uncomfortable truths which do not please public opinion, but which are necessary to safeguard the authentic good of society.

33. A specific priority is the need to examine and evaluate the predominant values and norms of modern society and culture in a Christian perspective, and the responsibility to try to communicate to society those *ethical and religious principles which give full meaning to human life.* In this way a university can contribute further to the development of a true Christian anthropology, founded on the person of Christ, which will bring the dynamism of the creation and redemp-

tion to bear on reality and on the correct solution to the problems of life.

34. The Christian spirit of service to others for the *promotion of social justice* is of particular importance for each Catholic university, to be shared by its teachers and developed in its students. The Church is firmly committed to the integral growth of all men and women.[32] The Gospel, interpreted in the social teachings of the Church, is an urgent call to promote "the development of those peoples who are striving to escape from hunger, misery, endemic diseases and ignorance; of those who are looking for a wider share in the benefits of civilization and a more active improvement of their human qualities; of those who are aiming purposefully at their complete fulfillment."[33] Every Catholic university feels responsible to contribute concretely to the progress of the society within which it works: For example, it will be capable for ways to make university education accessible to all those who are able to benefit from it, especially the poor or members of minority groups who customarily have been deprived of it. A Catholic university also has the responsibility, to the degree that it is able, to help to promote the development of the emerging nations.

35. In its attempts to resolve these complex issues that touch on so many different dimensions of human life and of society, a Catholic university will insist on cooperation among the different academic disciplines, each offering its distinct contribution in the search for solutions; moreover, since the economic and personal resources of a single institution are limited, cooperation in *common research projects* among Catholic universities, as well as with other private and governmental institutions, is imperative. In this regard, and also in what pertains to the other fields of the specific activity of a Catholic university, the role played by various national

23

and international associations of Catholic universities is to be emphasized. Among these associations the mission of the *International Federation of Catholic Universities,* founded by the Holy See,[34] is particularly to be remembered. The Holy See anticipates further fruitful collaboration with this federation.

36. Through programs of continuing education offered to the wider community, by making its scholars available for consulting services, by taking advantage of modern means of communication, and in a variety of other ways, a Catholic university can assist in making the growing body of human knowledge and a developing understanding of the faith available to a wider public, thus expanding university services beyond its own academic community.

37. In its service to society, a Catholic university *will relate especially to the academic, cultural and scientific world* of the region in which it is located. Original forms of dialogue and collaboration are to be encouraged between the Catholic universities and the other universities of a nation on behalf of development, of understanding between cultures and of the defense of nature in accordance with an awareness of the international ecological situation.

Catholic universities join other private and public institutions in serving the public interest through higher education and research; they are one among the variety of different types of institutions that are necessary for the free expression of cultural diversity, and they are committed to the promotion of solidarity and its meaning in society and in the world. Therefore they have the full right to expect that civil society and public authorities will recognize and defend their institutional autonomy and academic freedom; moreover, they have the right to the financial support that is necessary for their continued existence and development.

2. Pastoral Ministry

38. Pastoral ministry is that activity of the university which offers the members of the university community an opportunity to integrate religious and moral principles with their academic study and non-academic activities, *thus integrating faith with life.* It is part of the mission of the Church within the university, and is also a constitutive element of a Catholic university itself, both in its structure and in its life. A university community concerned with promoting the institution's Catholic character will be conscious of this pastoral dimension and sensitive to the ways in which it can have an influence on all university activities.

39. As a natural expression of the Catholic identity of the university, the university community *should give a practical demonstration of its faith in its daily activity,* with important moments of reflection and of prayer. Catholic members of this community will be offered opportunities to assimilate Catholic teaching and practice into their lives and will be encouraged to participate in the celebration of the sacraments, especially the Eucharist as the most perfect act of community worship. When the academic community includes members of other churches, ecclesial communities or religions, their initiatives for reflection and prayer in accordance with their own beliefs are to be respected.

40. Those involved in pastoral ministry will encourage teachers and students to become more aware of their responsibility toward those who are suffering physically or spiritually. Following the example of Christ, they will be particularly attentive to the poorest and to those who suffer economic, social, cultural or religious injustice. This responsibility begins within the academic community, but it also finds application beyond it.

41. Pastoral ministry is an indispensable means by which

Catholic students can, in fulfillment of their Baptism, *be prepared for active participation in the life of the Church;* it can assist in developing and nurturing the value of marriage and family life, fostering vocations to the priesthood and religious life, stimulating the Christian commitment of the laity and imbuing every activity with the spirit of the Gospel. Close cooperation between pastoral ministry in a Catholic university and the other activities within the local Church, under the guidance or with the approval of the diocesan bishop, will contribute to their mutual growth.[35]

42. Various associations or movements of spiritual and apostolic life, especially those developed specifically for students, can be of great assistance in developing the pastoral aspects of university life.

3. Cultural Dialogue

43. By its very nature, a university develops culture through its research, helps to transmit the local culture to each succeeding generation through its teaching, and assists cultural activities through its educational services. It is open to all human experience and is ready to dialogue with and learn from any culture. A Catholic university shares in this, offering the rich experience of the Church's own culture. In addition, a Catholic university, aware that human culture is open to Revelation and transcendence, is also a primary and privileged place for a *fruitful dialogue between the Gospel and culture.*

44. Through this dialogue a Catholic university assists the Church, enabling it to come to a better knowledge of diverse cultures, discern their positive and negative aspects, to receive their authentically human contributions, and to develop means by which it can make the faith better understood by the men and women of a particular culture.[36] While it is true that the

26

Gospel cannot be identified with any particular culture and transcends all cultures, it is also true that "the kingdom which the Gospel proclaims is lived by men and women who are profoundly linked to a culture, and the building up of the kingdom cannot avoid borrowing the elements of human culture or cultures."[37] "A faith that places itself on the margin of what is human, of what is therefore culture, would be a faith unfaithful to the fullness of what the Word of God manifests and reveals, a decapitated faith, worse still, a faith in the process of self-annihilation."[38]

45. A Catholic university must become *more attentive to the cultures of the world of today,* and to the *various cultural traditions existing within the Church* in a way that will promote a continuous and profitable dialogue between the Gospel and modern society. Among the criteria that characterize the values of a culture are, above all, the *meaning of the human person,* his or her liberty, dignity, *sense of responsibility,* and openness to the transcendent. To a respect for persons is joined *the preeminent value of the family,* the primary unit of every human culture.

Catholic universities will seek to discern and evaluate both the aspirations and the contradictions of modern culture, in order to make it more suited to the total development of individuals and peoples. In particular, it is recommended that by means of appropriate studies, the impact of modern technology and especially of the mass media on persons, the family, and the institutions and whole of modern culture be studied deeply. Traditional cultures are to be defended in their identity, helping them to receive modern values without sacrificing their own heritage, which is a wealth for the whole of the human family. Universities, situated within the ambience of these cultures, will seek to harmonize local cultures with the positive contributions of modern cultures.

46. An area that particularly interests a Catholic university is the *dialogue between Christian thought and the modern sciences*. This task requires persons particularly well versed in the individual disciplines and who are at the same time adequately prepared theologically, and who are capable of confronting epistemological questions at the level of the relationship between faith and reason. Such dialogue concerns the natural sciences as much as the human sciences which posit new and complex philosophical and ethical problems. The Christian researcher should demonstrate the way in which human intelligence is enriched by the higher truth that comes from the Gospel: "The intelligence is never diminished, rather, it is stimulated and reinforced by that interior fount of deep understanding that is the Word of God, and by the hierarchy of values that results from it.... In its unique manner, the Catholic university helps to manifest the superiority of the spirit, that can never, without the risk of losing its very self, be placed at the service of something other than the search for truth."[39]

47. Besides cultural dialogue, a Catholic university, in accordance with its specific ends, and keeping in mind the various religious-cultural contexts, following the directives promulgated by competent ecclesiastical authority, can offer a contribution to ecumenical dialogue. It does so to further the search for unity among all Christians. In interreligious dialogue it will assist in discerning the spiritual values that are present in the different religions.

4. Evangelization

48. The primary mission of the Church is to preach the Gospel in such a way that a relationship between faith and life is established in each individual and in the sociocultural context in which individuals live and act and communicate with

one another. Evangelization means "bringing the Good News into all the strata of humanity, and through its influence transforming humanity from within and making it new.... It is a question not only of preaching the Gospel in ever wider geographic areas or to ever greater numbers of people, but also of affecting and, as it were, upsetting, through the power of the Gospel, humanity's criteria of judgment, determining values, points of interest, lines of thought, sources of inspiration and models of life, which are in contrast with the Word of God and the plan of salvation."[40]

49. By its very nature, each Catholic university makes an important contribution to the Church's work of evangelization. It is a living *institutional* witness to Christ and his message, so vitally important in cultures marked by secularism, or where Christ and his message are still virtually unknown. Moreover, all the basic academic activities of a Catholic university are connected with and in harmony with the evangelizing mission of the Church: research carried out in the light of the Christian message which puts new human discoveries at the service of individuals and society; education offered in a faith-context that forms men and women capable of rational and critical judgment and conscious of the transcendent dignity of the human person; professional training that incorporates ethical values and a sense of service to individuals and to society; the dialogue with culture that makes the faith better understood, and the theological research that translates the faith into contemporary language. "Precisely because it is more and more conscious of its salvific mission in this world, the Church wants to have these centers closely connected with it; it wants to have them present and operative in spreading the authentic message of Christ."[41]

Part II:
General Norms

Article 1. The Nature of These General Norms

§1. These general norms are based on, and are a further development of, the Code of Canon Law[42] and the complementary Church legislation, without prejudice to the right of the Holy See to intervene should this become necessary. They are valid for all Catholic universities and other Catholic institutes of higher studies throughout the world.

§2. The general norms are to be applied concretely at the local and regional levels by episcopal conferences and other assemblies of Catholic hierarchy[43] in conformity with the Code of Canon Law and complementary Church legislation, taking into account the statutes of each university or institute and, as far as possible and appropriate, civil law. After review by the Holy See,[44] these local or regional "ordinances" will be valid for all Catholic universities and other Catholic institutes of higher studies in the region, except for ecclesiastical universities and faculties. These latter institutions, including ecclesiastical faculties which are part of a Catholic university, are governed by the norms of the apostolic constitution *Sapientia Christiana.*[45]

§3. A university established or approved by the Holy See, by an episcopal conference or another assembly of Catholic hierarchy, or by a diocesan bishop is to incorporate these general norms and their local and regional applications into its governing documents and conform its existing statutes both to the general norms and to their applications and submit them for approval to the competent ecclesiastical authority. It is contemplated that other Catholic universities, that is, those not established or approved in any of the above ways, with the agreement of the local ecclesiastical authority, will make their own the general norms and their local and regional applications, internalizing them into their governing documents, and, as far as possible, will conform their existing statutes both to these general norms and to their applications.

Article 2. The Nature of a Catholic University

§1. A Catholic university, like every university, is a community of scholars representing various branches of human knowledge. It is dedicated to research, to teaching, and to various kinds of service in accordance with its cultural mission.

§2. A Catholic university, as Catholic, informs and carries out its research, teaching and all other activities with Catholic ideals, principles and attitudes. It is linked with the Church either by a formal, constitutive and statutory bond or by reason of an institutional commitment made by those responsible for it.

§3. Every Catholic university is to make known its Catholic identity, either in a mission statement or in some other appropriate public document, unless authorized otherwise by the competent ecclesiastical authority. The university, particularly through its structure and its regulations, is to provide means which will guarantee the expression and the preservation of this identity in a manner consistent with Section 2.

§4. Catholic teaching and discipline are to influence all university activities, while the freedom of conscience of each person is to be fully respected.[46] Any official action or commitment of the university is to be in accord with its Catholic identity.

§5. A Catholic university possesses the autonomy necessary to develop its distinctive identity and pursue its proper mission. Freedom in research and teaching is recognized and respected according to the principles and methods of each individual discipline, so long as the rights of the individual and of the community are preserved within the confines of the truth and the common good.[47]

Article 3. The Establishment of a Catholic University

§1. A Catholic university may be established or approved by the Holy See, by an episcopal conference or another assembly of Catholic hierarchy, or by a diocesan bishop.

§2. With the consent of the diocesan bishop, a Catholic university may also be established by a religious institute or other public juridical person.

§3. A Catholic university may also be established by other ecclesiastical or lay persons; such a university may refer to itself as a Catholic university only with the consent of the competent ecclesiastical authority, in accordance with the conditions upon which both parties shall agree.[48]

§4. In the cases of Sections 1 and 2, the statutes must be approved by the competent ecclesiastical authority.

Article 4. The University Community

§1. The responsibility for maintaining and strengthening the Catholic identity of the university rests primarily with the university itself. While this responsibility is entrusted principally to university authorities (including, when the positions exist, the chancellor and/or a board of trustees or equivalent body), it is shared in varying degrees by all members of the university community and therefore calls for the recruitment of adequate university personnel, especially teachers and administrators, who are both willing and able to promote that identity. The identity of a Catholic university is essentially linked to the quality of its teachers and to respect for Catholic doctrine. It is the responsibility of the competent authority to watch over these two fundamental needs in accordance with what is indicated in Canon Law.[49]

§2. All teachers and all administrators, at the time of their appointment, are to be informed about the Catholic identity of the institution and its implications, and about their responsibility to promote, or at least to respect, that identity.

§3. In ways appropriate to the different academic disciplines, all Catholic teachers are to be faithful to, and all other teachers are to respect, Catholic doctrine and morals in their research and teaching. In particular, Catholic theologians, aware that they fulfill a mandate received from the Church, are to be faithful to the Magisterium of the Church as the authentic interpreter of Sacred Scripture and Sacred Tradition.[50]

§4. Those university teachers and administrators who belong to other churches, ecclesial communities, or religions as well as those who profess no religious belief, and also all students, are to recognize and respect the distinctive Catholic identity of the university. In order not to endanger the Catholic identity of the university or institute of higher studies, the number of non-Catholic teachers should not be allowed to constitute a majority within the institution, which is and must remain Catholic.

§5. The education of students is to combine academic and professional development with formation in moral and religious principles and the social teachings of the Church; the program of studies for each of the various professions is to include an appropriate ethical formation in that profession. Courses in Catholic doctrine are to be made available to all students.[51]

Article 5. The Catholic University Within the Church

§1. Every Catholic university is to maintain communion

with the universal Church and the Holy See; it is to be in close communion with the local Church and in particular with the diocesan bishops of the region or nation in which it is located. In ways consistent with its nature as a university, a Catholic university will contribute to the Church's work of evangelization.

§2. Each bishop has a responsibility to promote the welfare of the Catholic universities in his diocese and has the right and duty to watch over the preservation and strengthening of their Catholic character. If problems should arise concerning this Catholic character, the local bishop is to take the initiatives necessary to resolve the matter, working with the competent university authorities in accordance with established procedures[52] and, if necessary, with the help of the Holy See.

§3. Periodically, each Catholic university to which Article 3, Sections 1 and 2, refers, is to communicate relevant information about the university and its activities to the competent ecclesiastical authority. Other Catholic universities are to communicate this information to the bishop of the diocese in which the principal seat of the institution is located.

Article 6. Pastoral Ministry

§1. A Catholic university is to promote the pastoral care of all members of the university community, and to be especially attentive to the spiritual development of those who are Catholics. Priority is to be given to those means which will facilitate the integration of human and professional education with religious values in the light of Catholic doctrine, in order to unite intellectual learning with the religious dimension of life.

§2. A sufficient number of qualified people—priests, religious and lay persons—are to be appointed to provide pastoral ministry for the university community, carried on in harmony and cooperation with the pastoral activities of the local Church under the guidance or with the approval of the diocesan bishop. All members of the university community are to be invited to assist the work of pastoral ministry, and to collaborate in its activities.

Article 7. Cooperation

§1. In order better to confront the complex problems facing modern society, and in order to strengthen the Catholic identity of the institutions, regional, national and international cooperation is to be promoted in research, teaching and other university activities among all Catholic universities, including ecclesiastical universities and faculties.[53] Such cooperation is also to be promoted between Catholic universities and other universities, and with other research and educational institutions, both private and governmental.

§2. Catholic universities will, when possible and in accord with Catholic principles and doctrine, cooperate with government programs and the programs of other national and international organizations on behalf of justice, development and progress.

Transitional Norms

Article 8

The present Constitution will come into effect on the first day of the academic year 1991.

Article 9

The application of the Constitution is committed to the Congregation for Catholic Education, which has the duty to promulgate the necessary directives that will serve toward that end.

Article 10

It will be the competence of the Congregation for Catholic Education, when with the passage of time circumstances require it, to propose changes to be made in the present Constitution in order that it may be adapted continuously to the needs of Catholic universities.

Article 11

Any particular laws or customs presently in effect that are contrary to this Constitution are abolished. Also, any privileges granted up to this day by the Holy See, whether to physical or moral persons, that are contrary to this present Constitution are abolished.

Conclusion

The mission that the Church, with great hope, entrusts to Catholic universities holds a cultural and religious meaning of vital importance because it concerns the very future of humanity. The renewal requested of Catholic universities will make them better able to respond to the task of bringing the message of Christ to man, to society, to the various cultures:

"Every human reality, both individual and social has been liberated by Christ: persons, as well as the activities of men and women, of which culture is the highest and incarnate expression. The salvific action of the Church on cultures is achieved, first of all, by means of persons, families and educators…. Jesus Christ, our Savior, offers his light and his hope to all those who promote the sciences, the arts, letters and the numerous fields developed by modern culture. Therefore, all the sons and daughters of the Church should become aware of their mission and discover how the strength of the Gospel can penetrate and regenerate the mentalities and dominant values that inspire individual cultures, as well as the opinions and mental attitudes that are derived from it."[54]

It is with fervent hope that I address this document to all the men and women engaged in various ways in the significant mission of Catholic higher education.

Beloved brothers and sisters, my encouragement and my trust go with you in your weighty daily task that becomes ever more important, more urgent and necessary on behalf of evangelization for the future of culture and of all cultures. The Church and the world have great need of your witness and of your capable, free, and responsible contribution.

Given in Rome, at St. Peter's, on August 15, the solemnity of the Assumption of the Blessed Virgin Mary into heaven, in the year 1990, the 12th of the pontificate.

Joannes Paulus PP. II

Notes

1. Cf. the letter of Pope Alexander IV to the University of Paris, April 14, 1255, Introduction: *Bullarium Diplomatum...*, vol. III, Turin, 1858, p. 602.

2. St. Augustine, *Confessions,* X, xxiii, 33: "In fact, the blessed life consists in *the joy that comes from the truth,* since this joy comes from you who are Truth, God my light, salvation of my face, my God." *Patrologia Latina* 32, pp. 793-794. Cf. St. Thomas Aquinas, *De Malo,* IX, 1: "It is actually natural to man to strive for knowledge of the truth."

3. John Paul II, Discourse to the Catholic Institute of Paris, June 1, 1980: *Insegnamenti di Giovanni Paolo II,* Vol. 3/1 (1980), p. 1581.

4. John Paul II, Discourse to the Cardinals, November 10, 1979: *Insegnamenti di Giovanni Paolo II,* Vol. 2/2 (1979), p. 1096; cf. Discourse to UNESCO, Paris, June 2, 1980: *Acta Apostolicae Sedis,* 72 (1980), pp. 735-752.

5. Cf. John Paul II, Discourse to the University of Coimbra, May 15, 1982: *Insegnamenti di Giovanni Paolo II,* Vol. 5/2 (1982), p. 1692.

6. Paul VI, Allocution to Representatives of States, October 4, 1965: *Insegnamenti di Paolo VI,* Vol. 3 (1965), p. 508.

7. John Henry Cardinal Newman, *The Idea of a University,* (London: Longmans, Green and Company, 1931), p. XI.

8. Jn 14:6.

9. Cf. St. Augustine, *Serm.* 43, 9: PL 38, 258. Cf. also St. Anselm, *Proslogion,* Ch. 1: PL 158, 227.

10. Cf. John Paul II, Allocution to the International Congress on Catholic Universities, April 25, 1989, n. 3: AAS 18 (1989), p. 1218.

11. John Paul II, Apostolic Constitution *Sapientia Christiana,* concerning the Ecclesiastical Universities and Faculties, April 15, 1979: AAS 71 (1979), pp. 469-521.

12. Vatican Council II, Declaration on Catholic Education *Gravissimum Educationis,* n. 10: AAS 58 (1966), p. 737.

13. Mt 13:52.

14. Cf. *The Magna Carta of the European Universities,* Bologna, Italy, September 18, 1988, "Fundamental Principles."

15. Cf. Vatican Council II, Pastoral Constitution on the Church in the Modern World *Gaudium et Spes,* n. 59: AAS 58 (1966), p. 1080; Declaration on Catholic Education *Gravissimum Educationis,* n. 10: AAS 58 (1966), p. 737. "Institutional autonomy" means that the governance of an academic institution is and remains internal to the institution; "academic freedom" is the guarantee given to those involved in teaching and research that, within their specific spe-

cialized branch of knowledge and according to the methods proper to that specific area, they may search for the truth wherever analysis and evidence lead them, and may teach and publish the results of this search, keeping in mind the cited criteria, that is, safeguarding the rights of the individual and of society within the confines of the truth and the common good.

16. There is a twofold notion of *culture* used in this document: the *humanistic* and the *socio-historical*. "The word 'culture' in its general sense indicates all those factors by which man refines and unfolds his manifest spiritual and bodily qualities. It means his effort to bring the world itself under his control by his knowledge and his labor. It includes the fact that by improving customs and institutions he renders social life more human both within the family and in the civic community. Finally, it is a feature of culture that throughout the course of time man expresses, communicates and conserves in his works great spiritual experiences and desires, so that these may be of advantage to the progress of many, even of the whole human family. Hence it follows that human culture necessarily has a historical and social aspect and that the word 'culture' often takes on a sociological and ethnological sense." Vatican Council II, Pastoral Constitution on the Church in the Modern World *Gaudium et Spes,* n. 53: AAS 58 (1966), p. 1075.

17. "The Catholic University in the Modern World," final document of the Second International Congress of Delegates of Catholic Universities, Rome, November 20-29, 1972, Section 1.

18. *Ibid.*

19. John Paul II, Allocution to the International Congress on Catholic Universities, April 25, 1989, n. 4: AAS 81 (1989), p. 1219. Cf. also Vatican Council II, Pastoral Constitution on the Church in the Modern World *Gaudium et Spes,* n. 61: AAS 58 (1966), pp. 1081-1082. Cardinal Newman observes that a university "professes to assign to each study which it receives its proper place and its just boundaries; to define the rights, to establish the mutual relations and to effect the intercommunion of one and all" *(The Idea of a University,* p. 457).

20. Vatican Council II, Pastoral Constitution on the Church in the Modern World *Gaudium et Spes,* n. 36: AAS 58 (1966), p. 1054. To a group of scientists I pointed out that "while reason and faith surely represent two distinct orders of knowledge, each autonomous with regard to its own methods, the two must finally converge in the discovery of a single whole reality which has its origin in God" (John Paul II, *Address at the Meeting on Galileo,* May 9, 1983, n. 3: AAS 75 [1983], p. 690).

21. John Paul II, Address at UNESCO, June 2, 1980, n. 22: AAS 72 (1980), p. 750. The last part of the quotation uses words directed to the Pontifical Academy of Sciences, November 10, 1979: *Insegnamenti di Giovanni Paolo II,* Vol. 2/2 (1979), p. 1109.

22. Cf. Vatican Council II, Declaration on Catholic Education *Gravissimum Educationis,* n. 10: AAS 58 (1966), p. 737.

23. Vatican Council II, Pastoral Constitution on the Church in the Modern World *Gaudium et Spes,* n. 59: AAS 58 (1966), p. 1080. Cardinal Newman describes the ideal to be sought in this way: "A habit of mind is formed which lasts through life, of which the attributes are freedom, equitableness, calmness, moderation and wisdom" *(The Idea of a University,* pp. 101-102).

24. John Paul II, Post-Synodal Apostolic Exhortation *Christifideles Laici,* December 30, 1988, n. 44: AAS 81 (1989), p. 479.

25. Vatican Council II, Dogmatic Constitution on the Church *Lumen Gentium,* n. 31: AAS 57 (1965), pp. 37-38. Cf. Decree on the Apostolate of the Laity *Apostolicam Actuositatem, passim:* AAS 58 (1966), pp. 837ff. Cf. also *Gaudium et Spes,* n. 43: AAS 58 (1966), pp. 1061-1064.

26. Cf. Vatican Council II, Declaration on Religious Liberty *Dignitatis Humanae,* n. 2: AAS 58 (1966), pp. 930-931.

27. John Paul II, Address to Leaders of Catholic Higher Education, Xavier University of Louisiana, U.S.A., September 12, 1987, n. 4: AAS 80 (1988), p. 764.

28. Vatican Council II, Pastoral Constitution on the Church in the Modern World *Gaudium et Spes,* n. 59: AAS 58 (1966), p. 1080.

29. Cf. Vatican Council II, Dogmatic Constitution on Divine Revelation *Dei Verbum,* nn. 8-10: AAS 58 (1966), pp. 820-822.

30. Cf. Vatican Council II, Dogmatic Constitution on the Church *Lumen Gentium,* n. 25: AAS 57 (1965), pp. 29-31.

31. Cf. Congregation for the Doctrine of the Faith, "Instruction on the Ecclesial Vocation of the Theologian," May 24, 1990.

32. Cf. John Paul II, Encyclical Letter *Sollicitudo Rei Socialis,* nn. 27-34: AAS 80 (1988), pp. 547-560.

33. Paul VI, Encyclical Letter *Populorum Progressio,* n. 1: AAS 59 (1967), p. 257.

34. "Therefore, in that there has been a pleasing multiplication of centers of higher learning, it has become apparent that it would be opportune for the faculty and the alumni to unite in common association which, working in reciprocal understanding and close collaboration, and based upon the authority of the Supreme Pontiff, as father and universal doctor, they might more efficaciously spread and extend the light of Christ" (Pius XII, Apostolic Letter *Catholicas Studiorum Universitates,* with which the International Federation of Catholic Universities was established: AAS 42 [1950], p. 386).

35. The Code of Canon Law indicates the general responsibility of the bishop toward university students: "The diocesan bishop is to have serious pastoral concern for students by erecting a parish for them or by assigning priests for this purpose on a stable basis; he is also to provide for Catholic university centers at universities, even non-Catholic ones, to give assistance, especially spiritual, to young people" *(CIC,* can. 813).

36. "Living in various circumstances during the course of time, the Church, too, has used in her preaching the discoveries of different cultures to spread and explain the message of Christ to all nations, to probe it and more deeply understand it, and to give it better expression in liturgical celebrations and in the life of the diversified community of the faithful." (Vatican Council II, Pastoral Constitution on the Church in the Modern World *Gaudium et Spes,* n. 58: AAS 58 [1966], p. 1079).

37. Paul VI, Apostolic Exhortation *Evangelii Nuntiandi,* n. 20: AAS 68 (1976), p. 18. Cf. Vatican Council II, Pastoral Constitution on the Church in the Modern World *Gaudium et Spes,* n. 58: AAS 58 (1966), p. 1079.

38. John Paul II, Address to Intellectuals, Students and University Personnel at Medellin, Columbia, July 5, 1986, n. 3: AAS 79 (1987), p. 99. Cf. also Vatican Council II, Pastoral Constitution on the Church in the Modern World *Gaudium et Spes,* n. 58: AAS 58 (1966), p. 1079.

39. Paul VI, Address to the Delegates of the International Federation of Catholic Universities, November 27, 1972: AAS 64 (1972), p. 770.

40. Paul VI, Apostolic Exhortation *Evangelii Nuntiandi,* n. 18ff.: AAS 68 (1976) pp. 17-18.

41. Paul VI, Address to Presidents and Rectors of the Universities of the Society of Jesus, August 6, 1975, n. 2: AAS 67 (1975), p. 533. Speaking to the participants of the International Congress on Catholic Universities, April 25, 1989, I added (n. 5): "Within a Catholic university the evangelical mission of the Church and the mission of research and teaching become *interrelated* and *coordinated":* Cf. AAS 81 (1989), p. 1220.

42. Cf. in particular the Chapter of the Code: "Catholic Universities and Other Institutes of Higher Studies" (*CIC,* cann. 807-814).

43. Episcopal conferences were established in the Latin Rite. Other Rites have other assemblies of Catholic hierarchy.

44. Cf. *CIC,* Can. 455, Section 2.

45. Cf. *Sapientia Christiana:* AAS 71 (1979), pp. 469-521. Ecclesiastical universities and faculties are those that have the right to confer academic degrees by the authority of the Holy See.

46. Cf. Vatican Council II, Declaration on Religious Liberty *Dignitatis Humanae,* n. 2: AAS 58 (1966), pp. 930-931.

47. Cf. Vatican Council II, Pastoral Constitution on the Church in the Modern World *Gaudium et Spes,* nn. 57 and 59: AAS 58 (1966), pp. 1077-1080; *Gravissimum Educationis,* n. 10: AAS 58 (1966), p. 737.

48. Both the establishment of such a university and the conditions by which it may refer to itself as a Catholic university are to be in accordance with the prescriptions issued by the Holy See, episcopal conference or other assembly of Catholic hierarchy.

49. Canon 810 of CIC specifies the responsibility of the competent authorities in this area: Section 1: "It is the responsibility of the authority who is

competent in accord with the statutes to provide for the appointment of teachers to Catholic universities who, besides their scientific and pedagogical suitability, are also outstanding in their integrity of doctrine and probity of life; when those requisite qualities are lacking they are to be removed form their positions in accord with the procedure set forth in the statutes. Section 2: The conference of bishops and the diocesan bishops concerned have the duty and right of being vigilant that in these universities the principles of Catholic doctrine are faithfully observed." Cf. also Article 5, Section 2 ahead in these "Norms."

50. Vatican Council II, Dogmatic Constitution on the Church *Lumen Gentium,* n. 25: AAS 57 (1965), p. 29; *Dei Verbum,* nn. 8-10: AAS 58 (1966) pp. 820-822; cf. *CIC,* can. 812: "It is necessary that those who teach theological disciplines in any institute of higher studies have a mandate from the competent ecclesiastical authority."

51. Cf. *CIC,* can. 811, Section 2.

52. For universities to which Article 3, Sections 1 and 2, refer, these procedures are to be established in the university statutes approved by the competent ecclesiastical authority; for other Catholic universities, they are to be determined by episcopal conferences or other assemblies of Catholic hierarchy.

53. Cf. *CIC,* can. 820. Cf. also *Sapientia Christiana,* Norms of Application, Article 49: AAS 71 (1979), p. 512.

54. John Paul II, Address to the Pontifical Council for Culture, January 13, 1989, n. 2: AAS 81 (1989), pp. 857-858.